THE
PASSWORD
TRACKER & KEEPER

P A S S W O R D   B O O K

ACTIVINOTES

Activinotes

DAILY JOURNALS, PLANNERS, NOTEBOOKS AND OTHER BLANK BOOKS

WEBSITE URL: _____

USERNAME: _____

PASSWORD: _____

HINT: _____

NOTES: _____

_____

WEBSITE URL: _____

USERNAME: _____

PASSWORD: _____

HINT: _____

NOTES: _____

_____

WEBSITE URL: _____

USERNAME: _____

PASSWORD: _____

HINT: _____

NOTES: _____

_____

WEBSITE URL: _____

USERNAME: _____

PASSWORD: _____

HINT: _____

NOTES: _____

_____

WEBSITE URL: _____

USERNAME: _____

PASSWORD: _____

HINT: _____

NOTES: _____

_____

WEBSITE URL: _____

USERNAME: _____

PASSWORD: _____

HINT: _____

NOTES: _____

_____

WEBSITE URL: _____

USERNAME: _____

PASSWORD: _____

HINT: _____

NOTES: _____

_____

WEBSITE URL: _____

USERNAME: _____

PASSWORD: _____

HINT: _____

NOTES: _____

_____

_____

WEBSITE URL: _____

USERNAME: _____

PASSWORD: _____

HINT: _____

NOTES: _____

_____

WEBSITE URL: _____

USERNAME: _____

PASSWORD: _____

HINT: _____

NOTES: _____

_____

WEBSITE URL: _____

USERNAME: _____

PASSWORD: _____

HINT: _____

NOTES: _____

_____

WEBSITE URL: _____

USERNAME: _____

PASSWORD: _____

HINT: _____

NOTES: _____

_____

_____

WEBSITE URL: _____

USERNAME: _____

PASSWORD: _____

HINT: _____

NOTES: _____

_____

WEBSITE URL: _____

USERNAME: _____

PASSWORD: _____

HINT: _____

NOTES: _____

_____

WEBSITE URL: _____

USERNAME: _____

PASSWORD: _____

HINT: _____

NOTES: _____

_____

WEBSITE URL: _____

USERNAME: _____

PASSWORD: _____

HINT: _____

NOTES: _____

_____

_____

WEBSITE URL: _____

USERNAME: _____

PASSWORD: _____

HINT: _____

NOTES: _____

_____

WEBSITE URL: _____

USERNAME: _____

PASSWORD: _____

HINT: _____

NOTES: _____

_____

WEBSITE URL: _____

USERNAME: _____

PASSWORD: _____

HINT: _____

NOTES: _____

_____

WEBSITE URL: _____

USERNAME: _____

PASSWORD: _____

HINT: _____

NOTES: _____

_____

_____

WEBSITE URL: _____

USERNAME: _____

PASSWORD: _____

HINT: _____

NOTES: _____

_____

WEBSITE URL: _____

USERNAME: _____

PASSWORD: _____

HINT: _____

NOTES: _____

_____

WEBSITE URL: _____

USERNAME: _____

PASSWORD: _____

HINT: _____

NOTES: _____

_____

WEBSITE URL: _____

USERNAME: _____

PASSWORD: _____

HINT: _____

NOTES: _____

_____

_____

WEBSITE URL: _____

USERNAME: _____

PASSWORD: _____

HINT: _____

NOTES: _____

_____

WEBSITE URL: _____

USERNAME: _____

PASSWORD: _____

HINT: _____

NOTES: _____

_____

WEBSITE URL: _____

USERNAME: _____

PASSWORD: _____

HINT: _____

NOTES: _____

_____

WEBSITE URL: _____

USERNAME: _____

PASSWORD: _____

HINT: _____

NOTES: _____

_____

_____

WEBSITE URL: _____

USERNAME: _____

PASSWORD: _____

HINT: _____

NOTES: _____

_____

WEBSITE URL: _____

USERNAME: _____

PASSWORD: _____

HINT: _____

NOTES: _____

_____

WEBSITE URL: _____

USERNAME: _____

PASSWORD: _____

HINT: _____

NOTES: _____

_____

WEBSITE URL: _____

USERNAME: _____

PASSWORD: _____

HINT: _____

NOTES: _____

_____

_____

WEBSITE URL: _____

USERNAME: _____

PASSWORD: _____

HINT: _____

NOTES: _____

_____

WEBSITE URL: _____

USERNAME: _____

PASSWORD: _____

HINT: _____

NOTES: _____

_____

WEBSITE URL: _____

USERNAME: _____

PASSWORD: _____

HINT: _____

NOTES: _____

_____

WEBSITE URL: _____

USERNAME: _____

PASSWORD: _____

HINT: _____

NOTES: _____

_____

_____

WEBSITE URL: _____

USERNAME: _____

PASSWORD: _____

HINT: _____

NOTES: _____

_____

WEBSITE URL: _____

USERNAME: _____

PASSWORD: _____

HINT: _____

NOTES: _____

_____

WEBSITE URL: _____

USERNAME: _____

PASSWORD: _____

HINT: _____

NOTES: _____

_____

WEBSITE URL: _____

USERNAME: _____

PASSWORD: _____

HINT: _____

NOTES: _____

_____

_____

WEBSITE URL: _____

USERNAME: _____

PASSWORD: _____

HINT: _____

NOTES: _____

_____

WEBSITE URL: _____

USERNAME: _____

PASSWORD: _____

HINT: _____

NOTES: _____

_____

WEBSITE URL: _____

USERNAME: _____

PASSWORD: _____

HINT: _____

NOTES: _____

_____

WEBSITE URL: _____

USERNAME: _____

PASSWORD: _____

HINT: _____

NOTES: _____

_____

_____

WEBSITE URL: _____

USERNAME: _____

PASSWORD: _____

HINT: _____

NOTES: _____

_____

WEBSITE URL: _____

USERNAME: _____

PASSWORD: _____

HINT: _____

NOTES: _____

_____

WEBSITE URL: _____

USERNAME: _____

PASSWORD: _____

HINT: _____

NOTES: _____

_____

WEBSITE URL: _____

USERNAME: _____

PASSWORD: _____

HINT: _____

NOTES: _____

_____

_____

WEBSITE URL: _____

USERNAME: _____

PASSWORD: _____

HINT: _____

NOTES: _____

_____

_____

WEBSITE URL: _____

USERNAME: _____

PASSWORD: _____

HINT: _____

NOTES: _____

_____

_____

WEBSITE URL: _____

USERNAME: _____

PASSWORD: _____

HINT: _____

NOTES: _____

_____

_____

WEBSITE URL: _____

USERNAME: _____

PASSWORD: _____

HINT: _____

NOTES: _____

_____

_____

WEBSITE URL: _____

USERNAME: _____

PASSWORD: _____

HINT: _____

NOTES: _____

_____

WEBSITE URL: _____

USERNAME: _____

PASSWORD: _____

HINT: _____

NOTES: _____

_____

WEBSITE URL: _____

USERNAME: _____

PASSWORD: _____

HINT: _____

NOTES: _____

_____

WEBSITE URL: _____

USERNAME: _____

PASSWORD: _____

HINT: _____

NOTES: _____

_____

_____

WEBSITE URL: _____

USERNAME: _____

PASSWORD: _____

HINT: _____

NOTES: _____

_____

WEBSITE URL: _____

USERNAME: _____

PASSWORD: _____

HINT: _____

NOTES: _____

_____

WEBSITE URL: _____

USERNAME: _____

PASSWORD: _____

HINT: _____

NOTES: _____

_____

WEBSITE URL: _____

USERNAME: _____

PASSWORD: _____

HINT: _____

NOTES: _____

_____

_____

WEBSITE URL: _____

USERNAME: _____

PASSWORD: _____

HINT: _____

NOTES: _____

_____

WEBSITE URL: _____

USERNAME: _____

PASSWORD: _____

HINT: _____

NOTES: _____

_____

WEBSITE URL: _____

USERNAME: _____

PASSWORD: _____

HINT: _____

NOTES: _____

_____

WEBSITE URL: _____

USERNAME: _____

PASSWORD: _____

HINT: _____

NOTES: _____

_____

_____

WEBSITE URL: _____

USERNAME: _____

PASSWORD: _____

HINT: _____

NOTES: _____

_____

WEBSITE URL: _____

USERNAME: _____

PASSWORD: _____

HINT: _____

NOTES: _____

_____

WEBSITE URL: _____

USERNAME: _____

PASSWORD: _____

HINT: _____

NOTES: _____

_____

WEBSITE URL: _____

USERNAME: _____

PASSWORD: _____

HINT: _____

NOTES: _____

_____

_____

WEBSITE URL: _____

USERNAME: _____

PASSWORD: _____

HINT: _____

NOTES: _____

_____

WEBSITE URL: _____

USERNAME: _____

PASSWORD: _____

HINT: _____

NOTES: _____

_____

WEBSITE URL: _____

USERNAME: _____

PASSWORD: _____

HINT: _____

NOTES: _____

_____

WEBSITE URL: _____

USERNAME: _____

PASSWORD: _____

HINT: _____

NOTES: _____

_____

_____

WEBSITE URL: _____

USERNAME: _____

PASSWORD: _____

HINT: _____

NOTES: _____

_____

WEBSITE URL: _____

USERNAME: _____

PASSWORD: _____

HINT: _____

NOTES: _____

_____

WEBSITE URL: _____

USERNAME: _____

PASSWORD: _____

HINT: _____

NOTES: _____

_____

WEBSITE URL: _____

USERNAME: _____

PASSWORD: _____

HINT: _____

NOTES: _____

_____

_____

WEBSITE URL: _____

USERNAME: _____

PASSWORD: _____

HINT: _____

NOTES: _____

_____

WEBSITE URL: _____

USERNAME: _____

PASSWORD: _____

HINT: _____

NOTES: _____

_____

WEBSITE URL: _____

USERNAME: _____

PASSWORD: _____

HINT: _____

NOTES: _____

_____

WEBSITE URL: _____

USERNAME: _____

PASSWORD: _____

HINT: _____

NOTES: _____

_____

_____

WEBSITE URL: _____

USERNAME: _____

PASSWORD: _____

HINT: _____

NOTES: _____

_____

WEBSITE URL: _____

USERNAME: _____

PASSWORD: _____

HINT: _____

NOTES: _____

_____

WEBSITE URL: _____

USERNAME: _____

PASSWORD: _____

HINT: _____

NOTES: _____

_____

WEBSITE URL: _____

USERNAME: _____

PASSWORD: _____

HINT: _____

NOTES: _____

_____

_____

WEBSITE URL: _____

USERNAME: _____

PASSWORD: _____

HINT: _____

NOTES: _____

_____

WEBSITE URL: _____

USERNAME: _____

PASSWORD: _____

HINT: _____

NOTES: _____

_____

WEBSITE URL: _____

USERNAME: _____

PASSWORD: _____

HINT: _____

NOTES: _____

_____

WEBSITE URL: _____

USERNAME: _____

PASSWORD: _____

HINT: _____

NOTES: _____

_____

_____

WEBSITE URL: _____

USERNAME: _____

PASSWORD: _____

HINT: _____

NOTES: _____

_____

WEBSITE URL: _____

USERNAME: _____

PASSWORD: _____

HINT: _____

NOTES: _____

_____

WEBSITE URL: _____

USERNAME: _____

PASSWORD: _____

HINT: _____

NOTES: _____

_____

WEBSITE URL: _____

USERNAME: _____

PASSWORD: _____

HINT: _____

NOTES: _____

_____

_____

WEBSITE URL: _____

USERNAME: _____

PASSWORD: _____

HINT: _____

NOTES: _____

_____

WEBSITE URL: _____

USERNAME: _____

PASSWORD: _____

HINT: _____

NOTES: _____

_____

WEBSITE URL: _____

USERNAME: _____

PASSWORD: _____

HINT: _____

NOTES: _____

_____

WEBSITE URL: _____

USERNAME: _____

PASSWORD: _____

HINT: _____

NOTES: _____

_____

_____

WEBSITE URL: _____

USERNAME: _____

PASSWORD: _____

HINT: _____

NOTES: _____

_____

WEBSITE URL: _____

USERNAME: _____

PASSWORD: _____

HINT: _____

NOTES: _____

_____

WEBSITE URL: _____

USERNAME: _____

PASSWORD: _____

HINT: _____

NOTES: _____

_____

WEBSITE URL: _____

USERNAME: _____

PASSWORD: _____

HINT: _____

NOTES: _____

_____

_____

WEBSITE URL: _____

USERNAME: _____

PASSWORD: _____

HINT: _____

NOTES: _____

_____

WEBSITE URL: _____

USERNAME: _____

PASSWORD: _____

HINT: _____

NOTES: _____

_____

WEBSITE URL: _____

USERNAME: _____

PASSWORD: _____

HINT: _____

NOTES: _____

_____

WEBSITE URL: _____

USERNAME: _____

PASSWORD: _____

HINT: _____

NOTES: _____

_____

_____

WEBSITE URL: _____

USERNAME: _____

PASSWORD: _____

HINT: _____

NOTES: _____

_____

WEBSITE URL: _____

USERNAME: _____

PASSWORD: _____

HINT: _____

NOTES: _____

_____

WEBSITE URL: _____

USERNAME: _____

PASSWORD: _____

HINT: _____

NOTES: _____

_____

WEBSITE URL: _____

USERNAME: _____

PASSWORD: _____

HINT: _____

NOTES: _____

_____

_____

WEBSITE URL: _____

USERNAME: _____

PASSWORD: _____

HINT: _____

NOTES: _____

_____

WEBSITE URL: _____

USERNAME: _____

PASSWORD: _____

HINT: _____

NOTES: _____

_____

WEBSITE URL: _____

USERNAME: _____

PASSWORD: _____

HINT: _____

NOTES: _____

_____

WEBSITE URL: _____

USERNAME: _____

PASSWORD: _____

HINT: _____

NOTES: _____

_____

_____

WEBSITE URL: _____

USERNAME: _____

PASSWORD: _____

HINT: _____

NOTES: _____

_____

WEBSITE URL: _____

USERNAME: _____

PASSWORD: _____

HINT: _____

NOTES: _____

_____

WEBSITE URL: _____

USERNAME: _____

PASSWORD: _____

HINT: _____

NOTES: _____

_____

WEBSITE URL: _____

USERNAME: _____

PASSWORD: _____

HINT: _____

NOTES: _____

_____

_____

WEBSITE URL: _____

USERNAME: _____

PASSWORD: _____

HINT: _____

NOTES: _____

_____

WEBSITE URL: _____

USERNAME: _____

PASSWORD: _____

HINT: _____

NOTES: _____

_____

WEBSITE URL: _____

USERNAME: _____

PASSWORD: _____

HINT: _____

NOTES: _____

_____

WEBSITE URL: _____

USERNAME: _____

PASSWORD: _____

HINT: _____

NOTES: _____

_____

_____

WEBSITE URL: _____

USERNAME: _____

PASSWORD: _____

HINT: _____

NOTES: _____

_____

WEBSITE URL: _____

USERNAME: _____

PASSWORD: _____

HINT: _____

NOTES: _____

_____

WEBSITE URL: _____

USERNAME: _____

PASSWORD: _____

HINT: _____

NOTES: _____

_____

WEBSITE URL: _____

USERNAME: _____

PASSWORD: _____

HINT: _____

NOTES: _____

_____

_____

WEBSITE URL: _____

USERNAME: _____

PASSWORD: _____

HINT: _____

NOTES: _____

_____

WEBSITE URL: _____

USERNAME: _____

PASSWORD: _____

HINT: _____

NOTES: _____

_____

WEBSITE URL: _____

USERNAME: _____

PASSWORD: _____

HINT: _____

NOTES: _____

_____

WEBSITE URL: _____

USERNAME: _____

PASSWORD: _____

HINT: _____

NOTES: _____

_____

_____

WEBSITE URL: _____

USERNAME: _____

PASSWORD: _____

HINT: _____

NOTES: _____

_____

WEBSITE URL: _____

USERNAME: _____

PASSWORD: _____

HINT: _____

NOTES: _____

_____

WEBSITE URL: _____

USERNAME: _____

PASSWORD: _____

HINT: _____

NOTES: _____

_____

WEBSITE URL: _____

USERNAME: _____

PASSWORD: _____

HINT: _____

NOTES: _____

_____

_____

WEBSITE URL: _____

USERNAME: _____

PASSWORD: _____

HINT: _____

NOTES: _____

_____

WEBSITE URL: _____

USERNAME: _____

PASSWORD: _____

HINT: _____

NOTES: _____

_____

WEBSITE URL: _____

USERNAME: _____

PASSWORD: _____

HINT: _____

NOTES: _____

_____

WEBSITE URL: _____

USERNAME: _____

PASSWORD: _____

HINT: _____

NOTES: _____

_____

_____

WEBSITE URL: _____

USERNAME: _____

PASSWORD: _____

HINT: _____

NOTES: _____

_____

WEBSITE URL: _____

USERNAME: _____

PASSWORD: _____

HINT: _____

NOTES: _____

_____

WEBSITE URL: _____

USERNAME: _____

PASSWORD: _____

HINT: _____

NOTES: _____

_____

WEBSITE URL: _____

USERNAME: _____

PASSWORD: _____

HINT: _____

NOTES: _____

_____

_____

WEBSITE URL: _____

USERNAME: _____

PASSWORD: _____

HINT: _____

NOTES: _____

_____

WEBSITE URL: _____

USERNAME: _____

PASSWORD: _____

HINT: _____

NOTES: _____

_____

WEBSITE URL: _____

USERNAME: _____

PASSWORD: _____

HINT: _____

NOTES: _____

_____

WEBSITE URL: _____

USERNAME: _____

PASSWORD: _____

HINT: _____

NOTES: _____

_____

_____

WEBSITE URL: _____

USERNAME: _____

PASSWORD: _____

HINT: _____

NOTES: _____

_____

WEBSITE URL: _____

USERNAME: _____

PASSWORD: _____

HINT: _____

NOTES: _____

_____

WEBSITE URL: _____

USERNAME: _____

PASSWORD: _____

HINT: _____

NOTES: _____

_____

WEBSITE URL: _____

USERNAME: _____

PASSWORD: _____

HINT: _____

NOTES: _____

_____

_____

WEBSITE URL: _____

USERNAME: _____

PASSWORD: _____

HINT: _____

NOTES: _____

_____

WEBSITE URL: _____

USERNAME: _____

PASSWORD: _____

HINT: _____

NOTES: _____

_____

WEBSITE URL: _____

USERNAME: _____

PASSWORD: _____

HINT: _____

NOTES: _____

_____

WEBSITE URL: _____

USERNAME: _____

PASSWORD: _____

HINT: _____

NOTES: _____

_____

_____

WEBSITE URL: _____

USERNAME: _____

PASSWORD: _____

HINT: _____

NOTES: _____

_____

WEBSITE URL: _____

USERNAME: _____

PASSWORD: _____

HINT: _____

NOTES: _____

_____

WEBSITE URL: _____

USERNAME: _____

PASSWORD: _____

HINT: _____

NOTES: _____

_____

WEBSITE URL: _____

USERNAME: _____

PASSWORD: _____

HINT: _____

NOTES: _____

_____

_____

WEBSITE URL: _____

USERNAME: _____

PASSWORD: _____

HINT: _____

NOTES: _____

_____

WEBSITE URL: _____

USERNAME: _____

PASSWORD: _____

HINT: _____

NOTES: _____

_____

WEBSITE URL: _____

USERNAME: _____

PASSWORD: _____

HINT: _____

NOTES: _____

_____

WEBSITE URL: _____

USERNAME: _____

PASSWORD: _____

HINT: _____

NOTES: _____

_____

_____

WEBSITE URL: _____

USERNAME: _____

PASSWORD: _____

HINT: _____

NOTES: _____

_____

WEBSITE URL: _____

USERNAME: _____

PASSWORD: _____

HINT: _____

NOTES: _____

_____

WEBSITE URL: _____

USERNAME: _____

PASSWORD: _____

HINT: _____

NOTES: _____

_____

WEBSITE URL: _____

USERNAME: _____

PASSWORD: _____

HINT: _____

NOTES: _____

_____

_____

WEBSITE URL: _____

USERNAME: _____

PASSWORD: _____

HINT: _____

NOTES: _____

_____

WEBSITE URL: _____

USERNAME: _____

PASSWORD: _____

HINT: _____

NOTES: _____

_____

WEBSITE URL: _____

USERNAME: _____

PASSWORD: _____

HINT: _____

NOTES: _____

_____

WEBSITE URL: _____

USERNAME: _____

PASSWORD: _____

HINT: _____

NOTES: _____

_____

_____

WEBSITE URL: _____

USERNAME: _____

PASSWORD: _____

HINT: _____

NOTES: _____

_____

WEBSITE URL: _____

USERNAME: _____

PASSWORD: _____

HINT: _____

NOTES: _____

_____

WEBSITE URL: _____

USERNAME: _____

PASSWORD: _____

HINT: _____

NOTES: _____

_____

WEBSITE URL: _____

USERNAME: _____

PASSWORD: _____

HINT: _____

NOTES: _____

_____

_____

WEBSITE URL: _____

USERNAME: _____

PASSWORD: _____

HINT: _____

NOTES: _____

_____

WEBSITE URL: _____

USERNAME: _____

PASSWORD: _____

HINT: _____

NOTES: _____

_____

WEBSITE URL: _____

USERNAME: _____

PASSWORD: _____

HINT: _____

NOTES: _____

_____

WEBSITE URL: _____

USERNAME: _____

PASSWORD: _____

HINT: _____

NOTES: _____

_____

_____

WEBSITE URL: _____

USERNAME: _____

PASSWORD: _____

HINT: _____

NOTES: _____

_____

WEBSITE URL: _____

USERNAME: _____

PASSWORD: _____

HINT: _____

NOTES: _____

_____

WEBSITE URL: _____

USERNAME: _____

PASSWORD: _____

HINT: _____

NOTES: _____

_____

WEBSITE URL: _____

USERNAME: _____

PASSWORD: _____

HINT: _____

NOTES: _____

_____

_____

WEBSITE URL: _____

USERNAME: _____

PASSWORD: _____

HINT: _____

NOTES: _____

_____

WEBSITE URL: _____

USERNAME: _____

PASSWORD: _____

HINT: _____

NOTES: _____

_____

WEBSITE URL: _____

USERNAME: _____

PASSWORD: _____

HINT: _____

NOTES: _____

_____

WEBSITE URL: _____

USERNAME: _____

PASSWORD: _____

HINT: _____

NOTES: _____

_____

_____

WEBSITE URL: _____

USERNAME: _____

PASSWORD: _____

HINT: _____

NOTES: _____

_____

WEBSITE URL: _____

USERNAME: _____

PASSWORD: _____

HINT: _____

NOTES: _____

_____

WEBSITE URL: _____

USERNAME: _____

PASSWORD: _____

HINT: _____

NOTES: _____

_____

WEBSITE URL: _____

USERNAME: _____

PASSWORD: _____

HINT: _____

NOTES: _____

_____

_____

WEBSITE URL: _____

USERNAME: _____

PASSWORD: _____

HINT: _____

NOTES: _____

_____

WEBSITE URL: _____

USERNAME: _____

PASSWORD: _____

HINT: _____

NOTES: _____

_____

WEBSITE URL: _____

USERNAME: _____

PASSWORD: _____

HINT: _____

NOTES: _____

_____

WEBSITE URL: _____

USERNAME: _____

PASSWORD: _____

HINT: _____

NOTES: _____

_____

_____

WEBSITE URL: _____

USERNAME: _____

PASSWORD: _____

HINT: _____

NOTES: _____

_____

WEBSITE URL: _____

USERNAME: _____

PASSWORD: _____

HINT: _____

NOTES: _____

_____

WEBSITE URL: _____

USERNAME: _____

PASSWORD: _____

HINT: _____

NOTES: _____

_____

WEBSITE URL: _____

USERNAME: _____

PASSWORD: _____

HINT: _____

NOTES: _____

_____

_____

WEBSITE URL: _____

USERNAME: _____

PASSWORD: _____

HINT: _____

NOTES: _____

_____

WEBSITE URL: _____

USERNAME: _____

PASSWORD: _____

HINT: _____

NOTES: _____

_____

WEBSITE URL: _____

USERNAME: _____

PASSWORD: _____

HINT: _____

NOTES: _____

_____

WEBSITE URL: _____

USERNAME: _____

PASSWORD: _____

HINT: _____

NOTES: _____

_____

_____

WEBSITE URL: _____

USERNAME: _____

PASSWORD: _____

HINT: _____

NOTES: _____

_____

WEBSITE URL: _____

USERNAME: _____

PASSWORD: _____

HINT: _____

NOTES: _____

_____

WEBSITE URL: _____

USERNAME: _____

PASSWORD: _____

HINT: _____

NOTES: _____

_____

WEBSITE URL: _____

USERNAME: _____

PASSWORD: _____

HINT: _____

NOTES: _____

_____

_____

WEBSITE URL: _____

USERNAME: _____

PASSWORD: _____

HINT: _____

NOTES: _____

_____

WEBSITE URL: _____

USERNAME: _____

PASSWORD: _____

HINT: _____

NOTES: _____

_____

WEBSITE URL: _____

USERNAME: _____

PASSWORD: _____

HINT: _____

NOTES: _____

_____

WEBSITE URL: _____

USERNAME: _____

PASSWORD: _____

HINT: _____

NOTES: _____

_____

_____

WEBSITE URL: _____

USERNAME: _____

PASSWORD: _____

HINT: _____

NOTES: _____

_____

WEBSITE URL: _____

USERNAME: _____

PASSWORD: _____

HINT: _____

NOTES: _____

_____

WEBSITE URL: _____

USERNAME: _____

PASSWORD: _____

HINT: _____

NOTES: _____

_____

WEBSITE URL: _____

USERNAME: _____

PASSWORD: _____

HINT: _____

NOTES: _____

_____

WEBSITE URL: _____

USERNAME: _____

PASSWORD: _____

HINT: _____

NOTES: _____

_____

WEBSITE URL: _____

USERNAME: _____

PASSWORD: _____

HINT: _____

NOTES: _____

_____

WEBSITE URL: _____

USERNAME: _____

PASSWORD: _____

HINT: _____

NOTES: _____

_____

WEBSITE URL: _____

USERNAME: _____

PASSWORD: _____

HINT: _____

NOTES: _____

_____

_____

WEBSITE URL: _____

USERNAME: _____

PASSWORD: _____

HINT: _____

NOTES: _____

_____

WEBSITE URL: _____

USERNAME: _____

PASSWORD: _____

HINT: _____

NOTES: _____

_____

WEBSITE URL: _____

USERNAME: _____

PASSWORD: _____

HINT: _____

NOTES: _____

_____

WEBSITE URL: _____

USERNAME: _____

PASSWORD: _____

HINT: _____

NOTES: _____

_____

WEBSITE URL: _____

USERNAME: _____

PASSWORD: _____

HINT: _____

NOTES: _____

_____

WEBSITE URL: _____

USERNAME: _____

PASSWORD: _____

HINT: _____

NOTES: _____

_____

WEBSITE URL: _____

USERNAME: _____

PASSWORD: _____

HINT: _____

NOTES: _____

_____

WEBSITE URL: _____

USERNAME: _____

PASSWORD: _____

HINT: _____

NOTES: _____

_____

_____

WEBSITE URL: _____

USERNAME: _____

PASSWORD: _____

HINT: _____

NOTES: _____

_____

WEBSITE URL: _____

USERNAME: _____

PASSWORD: _____

HINT: _____

NOTES: _____

_____

WEBSITE URL: _____

USERNAME: _____

PASSWORD: _____

HINT: _____

NOTES: _____

_____

WEBSITE URL: _____

USERNAME: _____

PASSWORD: _____

HINT: _____

NOTES: _____

_____

_____

WEBSITE URL: _____

USERNAME: _____

PASSWORD: _____

HINT: _____

NOTES: _____

_____

WEBSITE URL: _____

USERNAME: _____

PASSWORD: _____

HINT: _____

NOTES: _____

_____

WEBSITE URL: _____

USERNAME: _____

PASSWORD: _____

HINT: _____

NOTES: _____

_____

WEBSITE URL: _____

USERNAME: _____

PASSWORD: _____

HINT: _____

NOTES: _____

_____

_____

WEBSITE URL: _____

USERNAME: _____

PASSWORD: _____

HINT: _____

NOTES: _____

_____

WEBSITE URL: _____

USERNAME: _____

PASSWORD: _____

HINT: _____

NOTES: _____

_____

WEBSITE URL: _____

USERNAME: _____

PASSWORD: _____

HINT: _____

NOTES: _____

_____

WEBSITE URL: _____

USERNAME: _____

PASSWORD: _____

HINT: _____

NOTES: _____

_____

_____

WEBSITE URL: _____

USERNAME: _____

PASSWORD: _____

HINT: _____

NOTES: _____

_____

WEBSITE URL: _____

USERNAME: _____

PASSWORD: _____

HINT: _____

NOTES: _____

_____

WEBSITE URL: _____

USERNAME: _____

PASSWORD: _____

HINT: _____

NOTES: _____

_____

WEBSITE URL: _____

USERNAME: _____

PASSWORD: _____

HINT: _____

NOTES: _____

_____

_____

WEBSITE URL: _____

USERNAME: _____

PASSWORD: _____

HINT: _____

NOTES: _____

_____

WEBSITE URL: _____

USERNAME: _____

PASSWORD: _____

HINT: _____

NOTES: _____

_____

WEBSITE URL: _____

USERNAME: _____

PASSWORD: _____

HINT: _____

NOTES: _____

_____

WEBSITE URL: _____

USERNAME: _____

PASSWORD: _____

HINT: _____

NOTES: _____

_____

_____

WEBSITE URL: _____

USERNAME: _____

PASSWORD: _____

HINT: _____

NOTES: _____

_____

WEBSITE URL: _____

USERNAME: _____

PASSWORD: _____

HINT: _____

NOTES: _____

_____

WEBSITE URL: _____

USERNAME: _____

PASSWORD: _____

HINT: _____

NOTES: _____

_____

WEBSITE URL: _____

USERNAME: _____

PASSWORD: _____

HINT: _____

NOTES: _____

_____

_____

WEBSITE URL: _____

USERNAME: _____

PASSWORD: _____

HINT: _____

NOTES: _____

_____

WEBSITE URL: _____

USERNAME: _____

PASSWORD: _____

HINT: _____

NOTES: _____

_____

WEBSITE URL: _____

USERNAME: _____

PASSWORD: _____

HINT: _____

NOTES: _____

_____

WEBSITE URL: _____

USERNAME: _____

PASSWORD: _____

HINT: _____

NOTES: _____

_____

_____

WEBSITE URL: _____

USERNAME: _____

PASSWORD: _____

HINT: _____

NOTES: _____

_____

WEBSITE URL: _____

USERNAME: _____

PASSWORD: _____

HINT: _____

NOTES: _____

_____

WEBSITE URL: _____

USERNAME: _____

PASSWORD: _____

HINT: _____

NOTES: _____

_____

WEBSITE URL: _____

USERNAME: _____

PASSWORD: _____

HINT: _____

NOTES: _____

_____

_____

WEBSITE URL: _____

USERNAME: _____

PASSWORD: _____

HINT: _____

NOTES: _____

_____

WEBSITE URL: _____

USERNAME: _____

PASSWORD: _____

HINT: _____

NOTES: _____

_____

WEBSITE URL: _____

USERNAME: _____

PASSWORD: _____

HINT: _____

NOTES: _____

_____

WEBSITE URL: _____

USERNAME: _____

PASSWORD: _____

HINT: _____

NOTES: _____

_____

_____

WEBSITE URL: _____

USERNAME: _____

PASSWORD: _____

HINT: _____

NOTES: _____

_____

WEBSITE URL: _____

USERNAME: _____

PASSWORD: _____

HINT: _____

NOTES: _____

_____

WEBSITE URL: _____

USERNAME: _____

PASSWORD: _____

HINT: _____

NOTES: _____

_____

WEBSITE URL: _____

USERNAME: _____

PASSWORD: _____

HINT: _____

NOTES: _____

_____

_____

WEBSITE URL: _____

USERNAME: _____

PASSWORD: _____

HINT: _____

NOTES: _____

_____

WEBSITE URL: _____

USERNAME: _____

PASSWORD: _____

HINT: _____

NOTES: _____

_____

WEBSITE URL: _____

USERNAME: _____

PASSWORD: _____

HINT: _____

NOTES: _____

_____

WEBSITE URL: _____

USERNAME: _____

PASSWORD: _____

HINT: _____

NOTES: _____

_____

_____

WEBSITE URL: _____

USERNAME: _____

PASSWORD: _____

HINT: _____

NOTES: _____

_____

WEBSITE URL: _____

USERNAME: _____

PASSWORD: _____

HINT: _____

NOTES: _____

_____

WEBSITE URL: _____

USERNAME: _____

PASSWORD: _____

HINT: _____

NOTES: _____

_____

WEBSITE URL: _____

USERNAME: _____

PASSWORD: _____

HINT: _____

NOTES: _____

_____

_____

WEBSITE URL: _____

USERNAME: _____

PASSWORD: _____

HINT: _____

NOTES: _____

_____

WEBSITE URL: _____

USERNAME: _____

PASSWORD: _____

HINT: _____

NOTES: _____

_____

WEBSITE URL: _____

USERNAME: _____

PASSWORD: _____

HINT: _____

NOTES: _____

_____

WEBSITE URL: _____

USERNAME: _____

PASSWORD: _____

HINT: _____

NOTES: _____

_____

_____

WEBSITE URL: _____

USERNAME: _____

PASSWORD: _____

HINT: _____

NOTES: _____

_____

WEBSITE URL: _____

USERNAME: _____

PASSWORD: _____

HINT: _____

NOTES: _____

_____

WEBSITE URL: _____

USERNAME: _____

PASSWORD: _____

HINT: _____

NOTES: _____

_____

WEBSITE URL: _____

USERNAME: _____

PASSWORD: _____

HINT: _____

NOTES: _____

_____

_____

WEBSITE URL: _____

USERNAME: _____

PASSWORD: _____

HINT: _____

NOTES: _____

_____

WEBSITE URL: _____

USERNAME: _____

PASSWORD: _____

HINT: _____

NOTES: _____

_____

WEBSITE URL: _____

USERNAME: _____

PASSWORD: _____

HINT: _____

NOTES: _____

_____

WEBSITE URL: _____

USERNAME: _____

PASSWORD: _____

HINT: _____

NOTES: _____

_____

_____

WEBSITE URL: _____

USERNAME: _____

PASSWORD: _____

HINT: _____

NOTES: _____

_____

WEBSITE URL: _____

USERNAME: _____

PASSWORD: _____

HINT: _____

NOTES: _____

_____

WEBSITE URL: _____

USERNAME: _____

PASSWORD: _____

HINT: _____

NOTES: _____

_____

WEBSITE URL: _____

USERNAME: _____

PASSWORD: _____

HINT: _____

NOTES: _____

_____

_____

WEBSITE URL: _____

USERNAME: _____

PASSWORD: _____

HINT: _____

NOTES: _____

_____

WEBSITE URL: _____

USERNAME: _____

PASSWORD: _____

HINT: _____

NOTES: _____

_____

WEBSITE URL: _____

USERNAME: _____

PASSWORD: _____

HINT: _____

NOTES: _____

_____

WEBSITE URL: _____

USERNAME: _____

PASSWORD: _____

HINT: _____

NOTES: _____

_____

WEBSITE URL: _____

USERNAME: _____

PASSWORD: _____

HINT: _____

NOTES: _____

_____

WEBSITE URL: _____

USERNAME: _____

PASSWORD: _____

HINT: _____

NOTES: _____

_____

WEBSITE URL: _____

USERNAME: _____

PASSWORD: _____

HINT: _____

NOTES: _____

_____

WEBSITE URL: _____

USERNAME: _____

PASSWORD: _____

HINT: _____

NOTES: _____

_____

_____

WEBSITE URL: _____

USERNAME: _____

PASSWORD: _____

HINT: _____

NOTES: _____

_____

WEBSITE URL: _____

USERNAME: _____

PASSWORD: _____

HINT: _____

NOTES: _____

_____

WEBSITE URL: _____

USERNAME: _____

PASSWORD: _____

HINT: _____

NOTES: _____

_____

WEBSITE URL: _____

USERNAME: _____

PASSWORD: _____

HINT: _____

NOTES: _____

_____

_____

WEBSITE URL: _____

USERNAME: _____

PASSWORD: _____

HINT: _____

NOTES: _____

_____

WEBSITE URL: _____

USERNAME: _____

PASSWORD: _____

HINT: _____

NOTES: _____

_____

WEBSITE URL: _____

USERNAME: _____

PASSWORD: _____

HINT: _____

NOTES: _____

_____

WEBSITE URL: _____

USERNAME: _____

PASSWORD: _____

HINT: _____

NOTES: _____

_____

_____

WEBSITE URL: _____

USERNAME: _____

PASSWORD: _____

HINT: _____

NOTES: _____

_____

WEBSITE URL: _____

USERNAME: _____

PASSWORD: _____

HINT: _____

NOTES: _____

_____

WEBSITE URL: _____

USERNAME: _____

PASSWORD: _____

HINT: _____

NOTES: _____

_____

WEBSITE URL: _____

USERNAME: _____

PASSWORD: _____

HINT: _____

NOTES: _____

_____

_____

WEBSITE URL: _____

USERNAME: _____

PASSWORD: _____

HINT: _____

NOTES: _____

_____

WEBSITE URL: _____

USERNAME: _____

PASSWORD: _____

HINT: _____

NOTES: _____

_____

WEBSITE URL: _____

USERNAME: _____

PASSWORD: _____

HINT: _____

NOTES: _____

_____

WEBSITE URL: _____

USERNAME: _____

PASSWORD: _____

HINT: _____

NOTES: _____

_____

_____

WEBSITE URL: _____

USERNAME: _____

PASSWORD: _____

HINT: _____

NOTES: _____

_____

WEBSITE URL: _____

USERNAME: _____

PASSWORD: _____

HINT: _____

NOTES: _____

_____

WEBSITE URL: _____

USERNAME: _____

PASSWORD: _____

HINT: _____

NOTES: _____

_____

WEBSITE URL: _____

USERNAME: _____

PASSWORD: _____

HINT: _____

NOTES: _____

_____

WEBSITE URL: _____

USERNAME: _____

PASSWORD: _____

HINT: _____

NOTES: _____

_____

WEBSITE URL: _____

USERNAME: _____

PASSWORD: _____

HINT: _____

NOTES: _____

_____

WEBSITE URL: _____

USERNAME: _____

PASSWORD: _____

HINT: _____

NOTES: _____

_____

WEBSITE URL: _____

USERNAME: _____

PASSWORD: _____

HINT: _____

NOTES: _____

_____

_____

WEBSITE URL: _____

USERNAME: _____

PASSWORD: _____

HINT: _____

NOTES: _____

_____

WEBSITE URL: _____

USERNAME: _____

PASSWORD: _____

HINT: _____

NOTES: _____

_____

WEBSITE URL: _____

USERNAME: _____

PASSWORD: _____

HINT: _____

NOTES: _____

_____

WEBSITE URL: _____

USERNAME: _____

PASSWORD: _____

HINT: _____

NOTES: _____

_____

_____

WEBSITE URL: _____

USERNAME: _____

PASSWORD: _____

HINT: _____

NOTES: _____

_____

WEBSITE URL: _____

USERNAME: _____

PASSWORD: _____

HINT: _____

NOTES: _____

_____

WEBSITE URL: _____

USERNAME: _____

PASSWORD: _____

HINT: _____

NOTES: _____

_____

WEBSITE URL: _____

USERNAME: _____

PASSWORD: _____

HINT: _____

NOTES: _____

_____

_____

WEBSITE URL: _____

USERNAME: _____

PASSWORD: _____

HINT: _____

NOTES: _____

_____

WEBSITE URL: _____

USERNAME: _____

PASSWORD: _____

HINT: _____

NOTES: _____

_____

WEBSITE URL: _____

USERNAME: _____

PASSWORD: _____

HINT: _____

NOTES: _____

_____

WEBSITE URL: _____

USERNAME: _____

PASSWORD: _____

HINT: _____

NOTES: _____

_____

WEBSITE URL: _____

USERNAME: _____

PASSWORD: _____

HINT: _____

NOTES: _____

_____

WEBSITE URL: _____

USERNAME: _____

PASSWORD: _____

HINT: _____

NOTES: _____

_____

WEBSITE URL: _____

USERNAME: _____

PASSWORD: _____

HINT: _____

NOTES: _____

_____

WEBSITE URL: _____

USERNAME: _____

PASSWORD: _____

HINT: _____

NOTES: _____

_____

_____

WEBSITE URL: _____

USERNAME: _____

PASSWORD: _____

HINT: _____

NOTES: _____

_____

WEBSITE URL: _____

USERNAME: _____

PASSWORD: _____

HINT: _____

NOTES: _____

_____

WEBSITE URL: _____

USERNAME: _____

PASSWORD: _____

HINT: _____

NOTES: _____

_____

WEBSITE URL: _____

USERNAME: _____

PASSWORD: _____

HINT: _____

NOTES: _____

_____

_____

WEBSITE URL: _____

USERNAME: _____

PASSWORD: _____

HINT: _____

NOTES: _____

_____

WEBSITE URL: _____

USERNAME: _____

PASSWORD: _____

HINT: _____

NOTES: _____

_____

WEBSITE URL: _____

USERNAME: _____

PASSWORD: _____

HINT: _____

NOTES: _____

_____

WEBSITE URL: _____

USERNAME: _____

PASSWORD: _____

HINT: _____

NOTES: _____

_____

_____

WEBSITE URL: _____

USERNAME: _____

PASSWORD: _____

HINT: _____

NOTES: _____

_____

WEBSITE URL: _____

USERNAME: _____

PASSWORD: _____

HINT: _____

NOTES: _____

_____

WEBSITE URL: _____

USERNAME: _____

PASSWORD: _____

HINT: _____

NOTES: _____

_____

WEBSITE URL: _____

USERNAME: _____

PASSWORD: _____

HINT: _____

NOTES: _____

_____

_____

WEBSITE URL: _____

USERNAME: _____

PASSWORD: _____

HINT: _____

NOTES: _____

_____

WEBSITE URL: _____

USERNAME: _____

PASSWORD: _____

HINT: _____

NOTES: _____

_____

WEBSITE URL: _____

USERNAME: _____

PASSWORD: _____

HINT: _____

NOTES: _____

_____

WEBSITE URL: _____

USERNAME: _____

PASSWORD: _____

HINT: _____

NOTES: _____

_____

_____

WEBSITE URL: _____

USERNAME: _____

PASSWORD: _____

HINT: _____

NOTES: _____

_____

WEBSITE URL: _____

USERNAME: _____

PASSWORD: _____

HINT: _____

NOTES: _____

_____

WEBSITE URL: _____

USERNAME: _____

PASSWORD: _____

HINT: _____

NOTES: _____

_____

WEBSITE URL: _____

USERNAME: _____

PASSWORD: _____

HINT: _____

NOTES: _____

_____

_____

WEBSITE URL: _____

USERNAME: _____

PASSWORD: _____

HINT: _____

NOTES: _____

_____

WEBSITE URL: _____

USERNAME: _____

PASSWORD: _____

HINT: _____

NOTES: _____

_____

WEBSITE URL: _____

USERNAME: _____

PASSWORD: _____

HINT: _____

NOTES: _____

_____

WEBSITE URL: _____

USERNAME: _____

PASSWORD: _____

HINT: _____

NOTES: _____

_____

_____

WEBSITE URL: _____

USERNAME: _____

PASSWORD: _____

HINT: _____

NOTES: _____

_____

WEBSITE URL: _____

USERNAME: _____

PASSWORD: _____

HINT: _____

NOTES: _____

_____

WEBSITE URL: _____

USERNAME: _____

PASSWORD: _____

HINT: _____

NOTES: _____

_____

WEBSITE URL: _____

USERNAME: _____

PASSWORD: _____

HINT: _____

NOTES: _____

_____

_____

WEBSITE URL: _____

USERNAME: _____

PASSWORD: _____

HINT: _____

NOTES: _____

_____

WEBSITE URL: _____

USERNAME: _____

PASSWORD: _____

HINT: _____

NOTES: _____

_____

WEBSITE URL: _____

USERNAME: _____

PASSWORD: _____

HINT: _____

NOTES: _____

_____

WEBSITE URL: _____

USERNAME: _____

PASSWORD: _____

HINT: _____

NOTES: _____

_____

_____

WEBSITE URL: _____

USERNAME: _____

PASSWORD: _____

HINT: _____

NOTES: _____

_____

WEBSITE URL: _____

USERNAME: _____

PASSWORD: _____

HINT: _____

NOTES: _____

_____

WEBSITE URL: _____

USERNAME: _____

PASSWORD: _____

HINT: _____

NOTES: _____

_____

WEBSITE URL: _____

USERNAME: _____

PASSWORD: _____

HINT: _____

NOTES: _____

_____

_____

WEBSITE URL: _____

USERNAME: _____

PASSWORD: _____

HINT: _____

NOTES: _____

_____

WEBSITE URL: _____

USERNAME: _____

PASSWORD: _____

HINT: _____

NOTES: _____

_____

WEBSITE URL: _____

USERNAME: _____

PASSWORD: _____

HINT: _____

NOTES: _____

_____

WEBSITE URL: _____

USERNAME: _____

PASSWORD: _____

HINT: _____

NOTES: _____

_____

_____

WEBSITE URL: _____

USERNAME: _____

PASSWORD: _____

HINT: _____

NOTES: _____

_____

WEBSITE URL: _____

USERNAME: _____

PASSWORD: _____

HINT: _____

NOTES: _____

_____

WEBSITE URL: _____

USERNAME: _____

PASSWORD: _____

HINT: _____

NOTES: _____

_____

WEBSITE URL: _____

USERNAME: _____

PASSWORD: _____

HINT: _____

NOTES: _____

_____

_____

WEBSITE URL: _____

USERNAME: _____

PASSWORD: _____

HINT: _____

NOTES: _____

_____

WEBSITE URL: _____

USERNAME: _____

PASSWORD: _____

HINT: _____

NOTES: _____

_____

WEBSITE URL: _____

USERNAME: _____

PASSWORD: _____

HINT: _____

NOTES: _____

_____

WEBSITE URL: _____

USERNAME: _____

PASSWORD: _____

HINT: _____

NOTES: _____

_____

_____

WEBSITE URL: _____

USERNAME: _____

PASSWORD: _____

HINT: _____

NOTES: _____

_____

WEBSITE URL: _____

USERNAME: _____

PASSWORD: _____

HINT: _____

NOTES: _____

_____

WEBSITE URL: _____

USERNAME: _____

PASSWORD: _____

HINT: _____

NOTES: _____

_____

WEBSITE URL: _____

USERNAME: _____

PASSWORD: _____

HINT: _____

NOTES: _____

_____

_____

WEBSITE URL: _____

USERNAME: _____

PASSWORD: _____

HINT: _____

NOTES: _____

_____

WEBSITE URL: _____

USERNAME: _____

PASSWORD: _____

HINT: _____

NOTES: _____

_____

WEBSITE URL: _____

USERNAME: _____

PASSWORD: _____

HINT: _____

NOTES: _____

_____

WEBSITE URL: _____

USERNAME: _____

PASSWORD: _____

HINT: _____

NOTES: _____

_____

_____

WEBSITE URL: _____

USERNAME: _____

PASSWORD: _____

HINT: _____

NOTES: _____

_____

WEBSITE URL: _____

USERNAME: _____

PASSWORD: _____

HINT: _____

NOTES: _____

_____

WEBSITE URL: _____

USERNAME: _____

PASSWORD: _____

HINT: _____

NOTES: _____

_____

WEBSITE URL: _____

USERNAME: _____

PASSWORD: _____

HINT: _____

NOTES: _____

_____

_____

WEBSITE URL: _____

USERNAME: _____

PASSWORD: _____

HINT: _____

NOTES: _____

_____

WEBSITE URL: _____

USERNAME: _____

PASSWORD: _____

HINT: _____

NOTES: _____

_____

WEBSITE URL: _____

USERNAME: _____

PASSWORD: _____

HINT: _____

NOTES: _____

_____

WEBSITE URL: _____

USERNAME: _____

PASSWORD: _____

HINT: _____

NOTES: _____

_____

_____

WEBSITE URL: _____

USERNAME: _____

PASSWORD: _____

HINT: _____

NOTES: _____

_____

WEBSITE URL: _____

USERNAME: _____

PASSWORD: _____

HINT: _____

NOTES: _____

_____

WEBSITE URL: _____

USERNAME: _____

PASSWORD: _____

HINT: _____

NOTES: _____

_____

WEBSITE URL: _____

USERNAME: _____

PASSWORD: _____

HINT: _____

NOTES: _____

_____

_____

WEBSITE URL: _____

USERNAME: _____

PASSWORD: _____

HINT: _____

NOTES: _____

_____

WEBSITE URL: _____

USERNAME: _____

PASSWORD: _____

HINT: _____

NOTES: _____

_____

WEBSITE URL: _____

USERNAME: _____

PASSWORD: _____

HINT: _____

NOTES: _____

_____

WEBSITE URL: _____

USERNAME: _____

PASSWORD: _____

HINT: _____

NOTES: _____

_____

_____

WEBSITE URL: _____

USERNAME: _____

PASSWORD: _____

HINT: _____

NOTES: _____

_____

WEBSITE URL: _____

USERNAME: _____

PASSWORD: _____

HINT: _____

NOTES: _____

_____

WEBSITE URL: _____

USERNAME: _____

PASSWORD: _____

HINT: _____

NOTES: _____

_____

WEBSITE URL: _____

USERNAME: _____

PASSWORD: _____

HINT: _____

NOTES: _____

_____

_____

WEBSITE URL: _____

USERNAME: _____

PASSWORD: _____

HINT: _____

NOTES: _____

_____

WEBSITE URL: _____

USERNAME: _____

PASSWORD: _____

HINT: _____

NOTES: _____

_____

WEBSITE URL: _____

USERNAME: _____

PASSWORD: _____

HINT: _____

NOTES: _____

_____

WEBSITE URL: _____

USERNAME: _____

PASSWORD: _____

HINT: _____

NOTES: _____

_____

_____

www.ingramcontent.com/pod-product-compliance
Lightning Source LLC
Chambersburg PA
CBHW081337090426
42737CB00017B/3189